AlwaysWondering

ALWAYS WONDERING

Some Favorite Poems of Aileen Fisher
Drawings by Joan Sandin

A Charlotte Zolotow Book
An Imprint of HarperCollins*Publishers*

ALWAYS WONDERING: Some Favorite Poems of Aileen Fisher
Text copyright © 1991 by Aileen Fisher
Illustrations copyright © 1991 by Joan Sandin
Typography by Anahid Hamparian
1   2   3   4   5   6   7   8   9   10
First Edition

Library of Congress Cataloging-in-Publication Data
Fisher, Aileen Lucia, date
   Always wondering / some favorite poems of Aileen Fisher ;
drawings by Joan Sandin.
      p.   cm.
   "A Charlotte Zolotow book."
   Includes index.
   Summary: The author selects some of the most requested poems
from her own work, grouped under such headings as "Think
About People," "Suddenly," and "Whoever Planned the World."
   ISBN 0-06-022851-2. — ISBN 0-06-022858-X (lib. bdg.)
   1. Children's poetry, American.   [1. American poetry.]
I. Sandin, Joan, ill.   II. Title.
PS3511.I7294A6   1991   90-23069
811'.52—dc20   CIP
                                                          AC

Other Books by Aileen Fisher

ANYBODY HOME?
EASTER
GOING BAREFOOT
I STOOD UPON A MOUNTAIN
LIKE NOTHING AT ALL
LISTEN, RABBIT
ONCE WE WENT ON A PICNIC
OUT IN THE DARK AND DAYLIGHT
RABBITS, RABBITS
SING, LITTLE MOUSE
WHEN IT COMES TO BUGS
THE HOUSE OF A MOUSE

CONTENTS

Think About People

Bird Talk

"Think . . ." said the robin,
"Think . . ." said the jay,
sitting in the garden,
talking one day.

"Think about people—
the way they grow:
they don't have feathers
at all, you know.

"They don't eat beetles,
they don't grow wings,
they don't like sitting
on wires and things."

"Think!" said the robin.
"Think!" said the jay.
"Aren't people funny
to be that way?"

Winter Birds

I can't go visit a snowbird—
I don't know where he stays.

I can't go visit a chickadee—
he has such flitty ways.

I can't go visit a blue jay
atop a snowy tree.

And so I scatter seeds around
and have them visit ME.

The Package

There's a package,
there's a package,
there's a package in the mail.
It's wrapped in yellow paper
and the twine is like a tail.
Three stamps are in the corner,
and the writing's rather pale—
there's a package,
there's a package,
there's a package in the mail.

It's for Mother,
it's for Mother,
it's for Mother, I can see,
but that is just about as good
as knowing it's for me,
for Mother'll say, "Come, open it,
untie the string and see."
There's a package,
there's a package,
oh, what CAN the package be?

Growing

When I ask Mother
she doesn't really know:
"What's inside of me
making me grow?"

So I ask Father,
who doesn't grow a bit:
"What's inside of *you*
making you quit?"

And Father says, "Hmmmmm.
I'm busy now, Son. . . ."
So I *still* don't know
how growing is done.

Walking

Father's legs are very long.
He seldom walks for fun.
He mostly walks for getting there,
which makes *me* have to run.

The Workshop

Father has a workshop
with a table and a scale
and a cupboard full of cubbies
for every kind of nail,
and a hammer and a hatchet
and an anvil and a brace . . .
and Father seems to know the minute
   things are out of place.

Father has a grindstone
that wobbles round and round,
and he has a sort of scraper
with a very scratchy sound,
and a wood rasp and a chisel
and a sickle for the lawn . . .
and Father seems to know the minute
   anything is gone!

Coffeepot Face

I saw
my face
in the coffeepot.

Imagine,
a COFFEEPOT FACE!

My eyes
were small
but my nose was not,

And my mouth
was . . . every place.

But Then

A tooth fell out
and left a space
so big my tongue
can touch my FACE.

And every time
I smile, I show
a space where some-
thing used to grow.

I miss my tooth,
as you may guess,
but then—I have to
brush one less.

Growing Up

When I grow up
(as everyone does)
what will become
of the Me I was?

Rain of Leaves

It's raining big,
it's raining small,
it's raining autumn leaves
in fall.

It's raining gold
and red and brown
as autumn leaves
come raining down.

It's raining everywhere
I look.
It's raining bookmarks
on my book!

After the End

After a book is finished,
don't you wish you knew
everything that happened
AFTER it was through?

First Day of School

I wonder
if my drawing
will be as good as theirs.

I wonder
if they'll like me
or just be full of stares.

I wonder
if my teacher
will look like Mom or Gram.

I wonder
if my puppy
will wonder
where I am.

My Cat

My cat rubs my leg
and starts to purr
with a soft little rumble,
a soft little whirr,
as if she had motors
inside of her.

I say, "Nice kitty,"
and stroke her fur,
and though she can't talk
and I can't purr,
she understands me,
and I do her.

After a Bath

After my bath
I try, try, try
to wipe myself
till I'm dry, dry, dry.

Hands to wipe
and fingers and toes
and two wet legs
and a shiny nose.

Just think how much
less time I'd take
if I were a dog
and could shake, shake, shake.

Who's Sleepy?

Who's sleepy?
Not me.
Who's sleepy?
Not *I*.
Not the owl in the tree,
the stars in the sky,
the bat on the wing,
the cat on the prowl,
the frog near the spring,
the dog with a howl.

Not the sickle of moon,
the trickle of water,
the skunk, the raccoon,
the mouse and her daughter.

Who's sleepy?
Not deer.
Not crickets I hear.
Not rabbits and such.
Not me . . .
         very much.

The World's So Big

Think of all the people
I'll never get to know
because the world's so big
and my wagon's so slow.

Think of all the places
I'll never get to see
because the street's so long
and Mother's calling me.

The Spinning Earth

The earth, they say,
spins round and round.
It doesn't look it
from the ground,
and never makes
a spinning sound.

And water never
swirls and swishes
from oceans full
of dizzy fishes,
and shelves don't lose
their pans and dishes.

And houses don't go whirling by,
or puppies swirl around the sky,
or robins spin instead of fly.

It may be true
what people say
about our spinning
night and day . . .
but I keep wondering
          anyway.

Until We Built a Cabin

When we lived in a city
(three flights up and down)
I never dreamed how many stars
could show above a town.

When we moved to a village
where lighted streets were few,
I thought I could see ALL the stars,
but, oh, I never knew . . .

Until we built a cabin
where hills are high and far,
I never knew how many
                many
                stars there really are.

Shooting Stars

When stars get loosened
in their sockets,
they shoot off through
the night like rockets.
But though I stay
and watch their trip
and search where they
have seemed to slip,
I never yet have found a CHIP
to carry in my pockets.

In the Country

I think people wonder
in the country much more
than they wonder in the city
with houses next door:

They see more world
in the country, more sky,
so there's much more space
for wondering. That's why.

Suddenly

Suddenly

Suddenly the shops are bright,
changed by magic overnight:
red and green against the white.

Suddenly the streets are gay
as the carols begin to play
up and down, across the way.

And the children, young and old,
ruddy with December cold,
SUDDENLY are good as gold.

December

I like days
with a snow-white collar,
and nights when the moon
is a silver dollar,
and hills are filled
with eiderdown stuffing
and your breath makes smoke
like an engine puffing.

I like days
when feathers are snowing
and all the eaves
have petticoats showing,
and the air is cold,
and the wires are humming,
but you feel all warm . . .
with Christmas coming.

Christmas Mouse

On the soft white snow
there's a thin white track
where a little mouse ran
but didn't come back . . .
for close to some rocks
where the tall weeds lean
the little mouse changed
to a submarine.

At the foot of a fir
he ducked down under—
does he live in a house
down there, I wonder,
with a wreath on his door
for his friends to see
and a sprig of spruce
for a Christmas tree?

Do Rabbits Have Christmas?

Do rabbits have Christmas,
I wonder, I wonder?
They have little spruces
to celebrate under,
where snow has made pompons
with silvery handles,
and frost has made tinsel
and icicle candles.

Do rabbits have presents,
I wonder, I wonder?
They have little fir trees
to celebrate under.
But do they have secrets
and smiles on their faces?
Let's go put some carrots
in rabbit-y places!

Christmas Tree

I'll find me a spruce
in the cold white wood
with wide green boughs
and a snowy hood.

I'll pin on a star
with five gold spurs
to mark my spruce
from the pines and firs.

I'll make me a score
of suet balls
to tie to my spruce
when the cold dusk falls,

And I'll hear next day
from the sheltering trees
the Christmas carols
of the chickadees.

Merry Christmas

I saw on the snow
when I tried my skis
the track of a mouse
beside some trees.
Before he tunneled
to reach his house
he wrote "Merry Christmas"
in white, in mouse.

Snow

Snow has magic
in its touch.
It makes the world
change very much:
it bends the hands
of spruces low
with fluffy
mittens-full of snow,
it turns the road
and house and yard
into a great big
Christmas card.

Valentines

I gave a hundred Valentines.
A hundred, did I say?
I gave a *thousand* Valentines
one cold and wintry day.

I didn't put my name on them
or any other words,
because my Valentines were seeds
for February birds.

Valentine's Day

The aspens and the maples now
have lacy frost on every bough.

And through the woods the shadows go,
writing verses on the snow.

The tops of weeds are sealed up
tight in little envelopes of white.

And listen! in the frosty pines
snowbirds twitter Valentines.

Easter Morning

We went out on an Easter morning
under the trees and the blue silk sky,
up to the hill where the buds were swelling—
Mother, Father, and Puck and I.

And I had hopes that we'd see a rabbit,
a brown little one with a cotton tail,
so we looked in the woods and under
    the bushes
and followed what seemed like a rabbit trail.

We peeked and poked. But there wasn't
    a rabbit
wherever we'd look, wherever we'd go.
And then I remembered, and said,
    "NO WONDER.
Easter's their busiest day, you know."

Time for Rabbits

"Look!" says the catkin
in its gray hatkin.
"Look!" say the larks and sparrows.
"The pasture is stirring,
the willows are purring,
and sunlight is shooting its arrows."

"Look!" wind is humming.
"Easter is coming.
Hear how the brooklet rushes.
It's time for the rabbits
with Easter-egg habits
to get out their paints and brushes."

On Mother's Day

On Mother's Day we got up first,
so full of plans we almost burst.

We started breakfast right away
as our surprise for Mother's Day.

We picked some flowers, then hurried back
to make the coffee—rather black.

We wrapped our gifts and wrote a card
and boiled the eggs—a little hard.

And then we sang a serenade,
which burned the toast, I am afraid.

But Mother said, amidst our cheers,
"Oh, what a big surprise, my dears.
I've not had such a treat in YEARS."
And she was smiling to her ears!

Halloween Concert

"It's cold," said the cricket,
"my fingers are numb.
I scarcely can fiddle,
I scarcely can strum.
And oh, I am sleepy
now summer has gone."
He dropped his fiddle
to stifle a yawn.

"Don't," said the field mouse, "act so sober.
You can't stop *yet*, when it's still October."

"I've played," said the cricket,
"for weeks and weeks.
My fiddle needs fixing—
it's full of squeaks.
My fingers need resting . . ."
He yawned. "Ho, hum,
I'm quite . . . (*yawn*) . . . ready
for winter to come.
I've found me the coziest,
doziest house . . ."

"You can't stop *now*," said his friend the mouse.
"You *can't*," said the mouse in a voice of sorrow,
"you can't desert us until tomorrow.
Tune up your fiddle for one last scene . . .
don't you remember it's HALLOWEEN?"

"What!" cried the cricket.
He yawned no more.
"You should have mentioned
the fact before.
Is everyone ready?
And where's the score?
What in the world
are we waiting for?"

The cricket fiddled,
the field mouse squeaked,
the dry weeds twiddled,
the bare twigs tweaked,
the hoot owl hooted,
the cornstalks strummed,
the west wind tooted,
the fence wires hummed.

Oh, what a concert all night long!
The fiddle was shrill and the wind was strong.
"Halloween, Halloween, crick, crack, creak.
Halloween, Halloween, scritch, scratch, squeak."

I Like Fall

I like fall:
it always smells smoky,
chimneys wake early,
the sun is poky,

Folks go past
in a hustle and bustle,
and when I scuff
in the leaves, they rustle.

I like fall:
all the hills are hazy,
and after a frost
the puddles look glazy,

And nuts rattle down
where nobody's living,
and pretty soon . . .
it will be THANKSGIVING.

When It's Thanksgiving

The kitchen's full of the nicest sounds:
of pans, and ladles stirring,
of bubbly pots, and kettles on,
and spoons and beaters whirring.

The kitchen's full of the finest smells:
of dinner in the making,
of turkey on, and cranberries,
and pumpkin pies a-baking.

The kitchen gives it all away
as sure as you are living—
you never have to LOOK at all
to know when it's Thanksgiving.

All in a Word

T for time to be together,
  turkey, talk, and tangy weather.
H for harvest stored away,
  home, and hearth, and holiday.
A for autumn's frosty art,
  and abundance in the heart.
N for neighbors, and November,
  nice things, new things to remember.
K for kitchen, kettles' croon,
  kith and kin expected soon.
S for sizzles, sights and sounds,
  and something special that abounds.

That spells THANKS—for joy in living
  and a jolly good Thanksgiving.

Such Things As These

Little Talk

Don't you think it's probable
that beetles, bugs, and bees
talk about a lot of things—
you know, such things as these:

The kind of weather where they live
in jungles tall with grass,
and earthquakes in their villages
whenever people pass.

Of course, we'll never know if bugs
talk very much at all—
because our ears are far too big
for talk that is so small.

Buried Treasure

How do squirrels remember,
when woods are white with snow,
where they hid the pine cones
they buried months ago?

Sometimes they remember
and sometimes they do *not*.
Look at all the seedlings
from cones the squirrels forgot!

Cat Bath

After she eats,
my purry friend
washes herself
from end to end.

Washes her face,
her ears, her paws,
washes the pink
between her claws.

I watch and think
it's better by far
to splash in a tub
with soap in a bar

And washcloth in hand
and towel on the rung
than to have to do all
that work BY TONGUE.

Fireflies

In the soft dark night
when the wind is still
and bullfrogs croak
at the bottom of the hill,
the fireflies reach
inside their coat pockets
and screw little light bulbs
into their sockets
so they can fly
through the night and play
without bumping their heads
or losing their way.

Baby Chick

Peck, peck, peck
on the warm brown egg.
Out comes a neck!
Out comes a leg!

How does a chick,
who's not been about,
discover the trick
of how to get out?

Spring Song

A meadowlark came back one day
and searched beneath the faded hay
out in the rocks, beside a cleft,
to find a song that he had left.

He found it. And he tried it out.
He tossed the melody about,
and not a note was hurt a bit
by winter drifting over it.

Spiders

Spiders are so sort-of-thin,
whatever do they keep it in—
the yards of thread they need to spin?

Snail's Pace

Maybe it's so
that snails are slow:
they trudge along and tarry.

But isn't it true
you'd slow up, too,
if you had a house to carry?

Horses

Back and forth
and up and down
horses' tails go switching.

Up and down
and back and forth
horses' skins go twitching.

Horses do
a lot of work
to keep themselves from itching.

As Soon As It's Fall

Rabbits and foxes
as soon as it's fall
get coats that are warm
with no trouble at all,
coats that are furry
and woolly and new,
heavy and thick
so the cold can't get through.

They don't have to buy them
or dye them or try them,
they don't have to knit them
or weave them or fit them,
they don't have to sew them
or stitch them all through . . .

They just have to GROW them,
and that's what they do.

Moles

Don't you feel sorry
for grubby old moles,
always in tunnels,
always in holes,
never out watching
the sun climb high
or the grass bend low
or the wind race by
or stars make twinkles
all over the sky?

A Little Bird

"What do you have for breakfast?"
I asked a little bird.
"Orange juice and cereal?"
He didn't say a word.
He merely ate a flower seed
and something from a limb—
which might, I guess, be cereal
and orange juice—for him!

Knowing

Nobody teaches
a bird to sing
or a frog to croak
as soon as it's spring.

Nobody teaches
a bee to make honey
or shows how-to-hop
to a new little bunny.

Nobody teaches
a spider to spin . . .
how do they know
what to do to BEGIN?

My Puppy

It's funny
my puppy
knows just how I feel:

When I'm happy
he's yappy
and squirms like an eel.

When I'm grumpy
he's slumpy
and stays at my heel.

It's funny
my puppy
knows such a great deal.

Bears

I wouldn't be a bear
for several reasons.

My main objection
has to do with seasons:

For one thing, I'd not like
hot fur in summer,

But then, I think the winters
would be dumber. . . .

Imagine! curling up where
there's no heating

And sleeping months and months
and never eating.

NEVER EATING!

Down in the Hollow

Down in the hollow,
not so far away,
I saw a little ladybug
when I went to play,
swinging on a clover
high in the air. . . .
I wonder if the ladybug
knew that I was there.

Butterfly Wings

How would it be
on a day in June
to open your eyes
in a dark cocoon,

And soften one end
and crawl outside,
and find you had wings
to open wide,

And find you could fly
to a bush or tree
or float on the air
like a boat at sea . . .

How would it BE?

Whoever
Planned
the World

Wise

Whoever planned
the world was wise
to think of land
and seas and skies,

To plan a sun
and moon that could
be made to run
the way they should.

But how did He
have time for all
the things we see
that are so small . . .

Like flowers in parks
and flakes of snow
and little sparks
the fireflies show?

Willow Cats

Spring, spring,
everything
you do is new and shiny.
Who, who
teaches you
to think of things as tiny
as all those velvet
willow cats
in furry coats
and furry hats
astride a twig
like acrobats,
soft, and sleek, and shiny?

Pussy Willows

Close your eyes
and do not peek
and I'll rub spring
across your cheek—
smooth as satin,
soft and sleek—
close your eyes
and do not peek.

Old Man Moon

The moon is very, very old.
The reason why is clear:
he gets a birthday once a month,
instead of once a year.

Comma in the Sky

A comma hung above the park,
a shiny punctuation mark;
we saw it curving in the dark
the night the moon was new.

A period hung above the bay,
immense though it was far away;
we saw it at the end of day
the night the moon was full.

Clouds

Wonder where they come from.
Wonder where they go.
Wonder why they're sometimes high
and sometimes hanging low.
Wonder what they're made of,
and if they weigh a lot.
Wonder if the sky feels bare
up there
             when clouds are *not*?

Fall

The last of October
we close the garden gate.
(The flowers have all withered
that used to stand straight.)

The last of October
we put the swings away.
The porch looks deserted
where we liked to play.

The last of October
the birds have all flown,
the screens are in the attic,
the sandpile's alone.

Everything is put away
before it starts to snow. . . .
I wonder if the ladybugs
have any place to go?

Autumn Leaves

One of the nicest beds I know
isn't a bed of soft white snow,
isn't a bed of cool green grass
after the noisy mowers pass,
isn't a bed of yellow hay
making me itch for half a day . . .
but autumn leaves in a pile THAT high,
deep, and smelling like fall, and dry.
That's the bed where I like to lie
and watch the flutters of fall go by.

The Seed

How does it know,
this little seed,
if it is to grow
to a flower or weed,
if it is to be
a vine or shoot,
or grow to a tree
with a long deep root?
A seed is so small,
where do you suppose
it stores up all
of the things it knows?

Seeds

Seeds know just the way to start—
I wonder how they get so smart.

They COULD come up in garden beds
feetfirst—by standing on their heads.

They COULD forget if they should grow
like sunflowers, high, or pumpkins, low.

They COULD forget their colors, too,
and yet they never, never do.

Package of Seeds

They can't see their pictures,
they can't read the label—
the seeds in a package—
so how are they able
to know if they're daisies
or greens for the table?

It sounds like a fancy,
it sounds like a fable,
but *you* do the sowing,
the weeding, the hoeing,
and *they'll* do the knowing
of how to be growing.

Windy Tree

Think of the muscles
a tall tree grows
in its leg, in its foot,
in its wide-spread toes—
not to tip over
and fall on its nose
when a wild wind hustles
and tussels and blows.

Weather

Weather is full
of the nicest sounds:
it sings
and rustles
and pings
and pounds
and hums
and tinkles
and strums
and twangs
and whishes
and sprinkles
and splishes
and bangs
and mumbles
and grumbles
and rumbles
and flashes
and CRASHES.

Open House

If I were a tree
I'd want to see
a bird with a song
on a branch of me.

I'd want a quick
little squirrel to run
up and down
and around, for fun.

I'd want the cub
of a bear to call,
and a porcupine, big,
and a tree toad, small.

I'd want a katydid
out of sight
on one of my leaves
to sing at night.

And down by my roots
I'd want a mouse
with six little mouselings
in her house.

Trees

Trees just stand around all day
and sun themselves and rest.

They never walk or run away,
and surely that is best

For otherwise how would a squirrel
or robin find its nest?

Wind

The wind has lots of noises:
it sniffs,
it puffs,
it whines,
it rumbles like an ocean
through junipers and pines,
it whispers in the windows,
it howls,
it sings,
it hums—
it tells you VERY PLAINLY
every time it comes.

The Sun

Every day coming,
every day going,
bringing a goldness
out of the black,

Every day climbing
over the heavens,
sinking at sunset,
soon to be back.

Coming and going,
going and coming,
leaving no footprint,
leaving no track.

Rain

How does
the rain
have the sense
to know
winter is here
and it's time
to snow?

November

Bracken on the hillside
frosted and white.
Garden all brown.
Storm windows tight.
Screens in the attic.
Barn full of hay.
Bathing suits mothproofed,
folded away.
And coming 'round the corner
on his tip, tip toes,
Winter, Winter, Winter
with a cold red nose.

Snow Color

I used to think
that snow was white.
And then
I saw it blue one night.

And then
I saw it gold one day,
with purple shadows
and with gray.

And then
one morning it was PINK.
So now
I don't know *what* to think.

Snowball Wind

The wind was throwing snowballs.
It plucked them from the trees
and tossed them all around the woods
as boldly as you please.

I ducked beneath the spruces,
which didn't help a speck:
the wind kept throwing snowballs
and threw one down my neck.

Hayfield

I like to see the wind
go racing through the hay:
it's just like a green fire
galloping away.
It's a field full of green flames
licking at the hill.
And then it's just a hayfield
... when the wind is still.

I like to see the wind
go swelling through the grass:
it's just like an ocean
when the green waves pass.
It's a green sea of billows
rolling toward the town.
And then it's just a hayfield
... when the wind dies down.

A Garden

We wanted a garden,
and oh, what fun
to plan a garden and dig in one.

But it was awful
the way the weeds
grew every place we planted seeds.

And it was frightful
how rain and such
was either too little or else too much.

But it was jolly
the day we spied
little green pods growing peas inside.

Grass

Do you ever think about grass
on the lawns you pass?
The green of it,
the sheen of it,
the after-raining clean of it
when it sparkles like glass?

Do you know what grass is,
those green spears showing
wherever you're going?

Every blade, to be brief,
is a *leaf*
without a twig, without a bough.
You never thought lawn mowers
went around
clipping leaves off the ground,
did you now?

On Time

"Set your watch," the weather said.
"See those doings up ahead—
stirrings in the crocus bed,
bluebirds on the wing,
sun a ball of golden thread,
maple tips a-swelling red.
Set your watch," the weather said,
"half a tick to spring!"

Flowers at Night

Some flowers close their petals,
blue and red and bright,
and go to sleep all tucked away
inside themselves at night.

Some flowers leave their petals
like windows open wide
so they can watch the goings-on
of stars and things outside.

Always Wondering

Roads run by
and paths run by
and tracks
where trains go thundering

Past green and brown
of field and town
and over-ing and under-ing.

Brooks run by
and creeks run by
and rivers
big and blundering,

And where they end,
around what bend,
I'm always, always wondering.